A job for Jordan

Written by Gill Munton

Speed Sounds

Consonants *Ask children to say the sounds.*

f ff ph	l ll le	m mm mb	n nn kn	r rr wr	s ss se c ce	v ve	z zz (se) s	sh	th	ng nk

b bb	c k ck	d dd	g gg	h	j g ge	p pp	qu	t tt	w wh	x	y	(ch) tch

Each box contains one sound but sometimes more than one grapheme.
*Focus graphemes for this story are **circled**.*

Vowels

Ask children to say the sounds in and out of order.

a	e	i	o	u	ay	ee	igh	ow
	ea				a-e	ea	i-e	o-e
						y	ie	o
						e	i	
at	hen	in	on	up	day	see	high	blow

oo	oo	ar	or	air	ir	ou	oy
u-e			oor	are	ur		oi
ue			ore		er		
			aw				
zoo	look	car	for	fair	whirl	shout	boy

Story Green Words

Ask children to read the words first in Fred Talk and then say the word.

Mark   Dawn   dog   pup   read   born   lead   each   lie down   worn   deal   act   team   sight   floor   speak   guide*

Ask children to say the syllables and then read the whole word.

Jor|dan   Lab|ra|dor   re|port   be|have   af|ter   har|ness   comm|and   own|er   traff|ic   un|til   spon|sor   supp|ort   web|site   be|cause*

Ask children to read the root first and then the whole word with the suffix.

train → trained   paw → paws   lesson → lessons

bump → bumping

*Challenge Words

Vocabulary Check

Discuss the meaning (as used in the non-fiction text) after the children have read the word.

	definition
guide dog	*a dog that helps someone who cannot see or hear well*
Labrador	*a medium-sized, friendly type of dog*
report	*writing that tells you about something*
harness	*a set of straps that goes over a dog's head to help you control the dog*
sponsor	*promise to give money*
website	*a place on the Internet where you can find information*

Red Words

Ask children to practise reading the words across the rows, down the columns and in and out of order clearly and quickly.

all	are	come	do
some	they	to	want
who	you	great	other
bought	could	everyone	what
should	whole	thought	watch

Mark needs his guide dog, Dawn, because he has poor sight.

A Labrador is a good sort of dog for this.

Read this report about how Jordan, a Labrador pup, is trained to be a guide dog.

All pups can be playful, but a guide dog pup has to behave. His owner's life will be in his hands – or his paws!

6 to 8 weeks after Jordan is born, he is taken out on a lead each morning to be trained.

A guide dog is trained to:

- sit
- lie down
- stay
- come.

When he is 1, a harness is worn by the pup.

He is trained in some more important lessons:

- how to stop before crossing a street
- how to go left or right on command
- how to stop his owner bumping into things
- how to deal with traffic.

Next, the guide dog meets his owner.

They are shown how to act as a team.

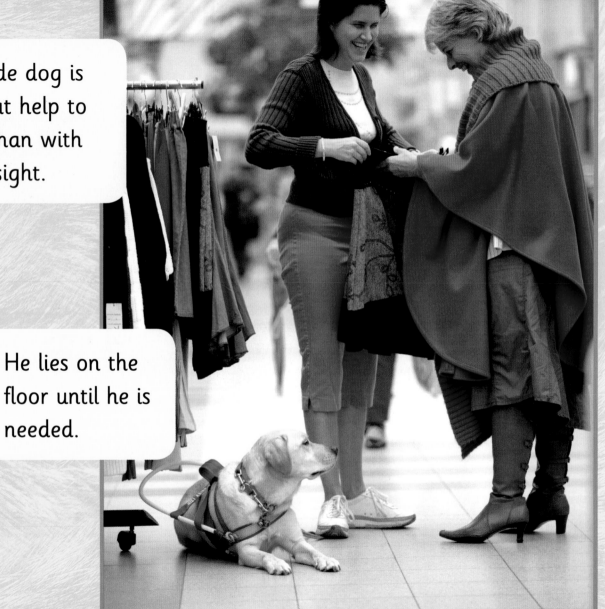

A guide dog is a great help to a woman with poor sight.

He lies on the floor until he is needed.

Do you want to sponsor a guide dog pup?

£1 a week will support a pup who is being trained to be a guide dog.

With an adult, go to this website if you want to know more: www.guidedogs.org.uk

Questions to talk about

Ask children to TTYP for each question using 'Fastest finger' (FF) or 'Have a think' (HaT).

p.9 (FF) What sort of dog makes a good guide dog?

p.10 (FF) When does Jordan's training start?

p.11 (FF) What is a guide dog trained to do?

p.12 (FF) At what age does a guide dog start to wear a harness?

p.13 (HaT) Why do a guide dog and his owner need to act as a team?

p.14 (FF) What does Jordan do when he is not needed?

p.15 (HaT) Why shouldn't you pat or speak to a guide dog?

Questions to read and answer

(Children complete without your help.)

1. Who is Dawn?

2. Why do you think Jordan is trained to stop before crossing a street?

3. What is worn by a guide dog when he is 1?

4. How much money a week will support a pup who is being trained?

5. Where can you find more information about dogs like Jordan?